THE POETRY BUS

Wonderful Words

Edited By Jenni Harrison

First published in Great Britain in 2022 by:

YoungWriters® Est. 1991

Young Writers
Remus House
Coltsfoot Drive
Peterborough
PE2 9BF
Telephone: 01733 890066
Website: www.youngwriters.co.uk

All Rights Reserved
Book Design by Ashley Janson
© Copyright Contributors 2021
Softback ISBN 978-1-80015-744-6

Printed and bound in the UK by BookPrintingUK
Website: www.bookprintinguk.com
YB0492C

Foreword

Welcome to a fun-filled book of poems!

Here at Young Writers, we are delighted to introduce our new poetry competition for KS1 pupils, The Poetry Bus. Pupils could choose to write an acrostic, sense poem or riddle to introduce them to the world of poetry. Giving them this framework allowed the young writers to open their imaginations to a range of topics of their choice, and encouraged them to include other literary techniques such as similes and description.

From family and friends, to animals and places, these pupils have shaped and crafted their ideas brilliantly, showcasing their budding creativity in verse.

We live and breathe creativity here at Young Writers – it gives us life! We want to pass our love of the written word onto the next generation and what better way to do that than to celebrate their writing by publishing it in a book!

Each awesome little poet in this book should be super proud of themselves, and now they've got proof of their imagination and their ideas when they first started creative writing to look back on in years to come! We hope you will delight in these poems as much as we have.

Contents

Barcroft Primary School, Barcroft

Marcie-Rae Moore (6)	1
Hannah Smith, Amolar, Keagan & Zain	2
Sahid Mohamed (6)	3
Louie Porter (7)	4
Amy Fox (7), Jayden, Codie & Charlie	5
Amarpreet Singh Dhillon (6)	6
Charley Jay Nutting (7)	7
Sol Simpson-Pratt (7)	8
Dylan Carless (6)	9
Zahara Lewis-Coombs (7)	10
Elsie Richardson (7)	11
Lottie Parkes (6)	12
Hannah Connell (6)	13
Tyler Evans (7)	14
Danielle Ansere (7)	15
Rhylee Yeend (8)	16
Kal Read (6)	17
Logan Olivier (7)	18
Olivia Smith (6)	19
Jack Grainger (6)	20
Dedan Abdullah (7)	21
Keiton Durbin (7)	22
Frankie Rathbone (7)	23
Juvraj Nijjar (6)	24
Carson Tipper (6)	25
Ethan Hirst (7)	26
Avnit Kaur (6)	27
Aston Spittle (7)	28
Lexi-Mae Dams-Jesson (7)	29
Amelia Zaman (6)	30
Leo Short (6)	31
Paige Barham (6)	32
Thomas Watkiss (7)	33
Sanaz Nahavandi-Nejad (6)	34
Alexandra Tolley (6)	35
Junior Smith (6)	36
Mia Rattu (6)	37
Layliia Bolding (6)	38
Bobby Guy (6)	39
Casey Richards (6), Chahat & Cruz	40

Bishops Itchington Primary School, Bishops Itchington

Amber Warren (6)	41
Flynn Boothe (6)	42
Orri Wiles (7)	43
Tia Hampson (7)	44
Arlo Nateghi (6)	45
Justina Tagg-Wilkinson (6)	46
Emily Cooper (6)	47
Josh Rycroft (6)	48
Austin Jenkins (6)	49
Benjamin Watson (7)	50
Ben Allen (7)	51
Emily Mann (6)	52
Iris Coleman (7)	53
Sophie Abbott (6)	54
Jacob Brooks (6)	55
Mason Brooks (6)	56

Hollinsclough CE Academy, Buxton

River Ackerman (6)	57
Aliza Mottram (5)	58
Bella Ferns (7)	59

River Whorton (7)	60
Eva Gardham (7)	61
Rory Wale (6)	62
Caleb Bates (5)	63
Buddy Searle (5)	64
Lochie Dunne-Larsen (7)	65
Molly Marsh (8)	66
Bruno Searle (6)	67
Harry Lager (7)	68
Indigo Grindon (6)	69
Hendrix Sutherland (5)	70
Dylan Sutherland (7)	71
Rosalie Whorton (7)	72

Malvern Parish CE Primary School, Malvern

Amélie Hutchinson (6)	73
Edie Morse (7)	74
Hannah Nealon (6)	75
Rosie Kelland (6)	76
Jamie Atkins (6)	77
Emily Lewis (7)	78
Andrew Marlow (6)	79
Abigail Whiteman (6)	80
George Collier (6)	81
Edith Dolphin (6)	82
Estella Nutt (6)	83
Élodie Argent (6)	84
Hugo Sherman (6)	85
Kourtney-Jai Thackeray (7)	86
Jenson Iley (6)	87
James Roberts-Haggis (7)	88
Teddy Smith (6)	89
Katherine Buckman (6)	90
Poppy Morris (6)	91
Josie-May Jones (6)	92
Jacob Davies (6)	93

Ormiston Cliff Park Primary Academy, Gorleston

Leonidas McNally (6)	94
Oreoluwa Odyneye (6)	95
Abdul Ahad (6)	96
Marnie Rudkin (7)	97
Lyla Puszczewicz (6)	98
Ross Vaudin (6)	99
Yalini Manivannan (6)	100
Henry Cutchey (6)	101
Harper Leigh (6)	102
Lewis Wright (6)	103
Iris Rogers	104
Mason Sandry (6)	105
Freddie Roden (6)	106
Jenson Brooks (6)	107
Joanna Mercy Jomy (6)	108
Isaac Bartram (6)	109
Roma Down (7)	110
Leon Quelch	111
Thomas Russell (6)	112
Grace Chance (7)	113
Anna Haziri (6)	114
Ezmai Doroba (6)	115
Sienna (6)	116
Nour Genena (6)	117
Arya Vikramraj (6)	118
Maya Adams (6)	119
Malwina	120
Toby Rix (6)	121
Elsie Smith (6)	122
Link Mitchell (6)	123
Beau Learmonth (6)	124
Charliee Louise Down (6)	125
Frankie Potter (6)	126
Evie Redmond (6)	127
Ezmai Eaton (6)	128
Nicola Anne (6)	129
Yusuf Kadar (6)	130

Our Lady & St Joseph RC Primary School, Hackney

Annalise Campbell (6)	131
Tehillah Sodunke (6)	132
Luca Chiromo (6)	133
Eabha Enver (6)	134
Elijah Mckenzie (7)	135
Elijah Gomez (6)	136
Ivy Neave (6)	137
Haviliah Ojarikre (6)	138
Evie Doyle (6)	139
Luca Nguyen-Finer (7)	140
Eliott Arnoux (7)	141
Niamh Buck (7)	142
Nathaniel Mullings-Khan (6)	143
Luca Grossi (6)	144
Sienna Monero (6)	145
Janelle Alexander (6)	146

Ribbleton Avenue Infant School, Preston

Abdullah Khan (6)	147
Lewis Nuttall (6)	148

The Poems

My Bonfire Night Poem

B onfire Night brings people together
O n Bonfire Night it's magical
N ever go near the fire
F ireworks are dangerous because they burn your hands
I like Bonfire Night because it's special
R ed is my favourite colour because it's light
E verybody celebrates Bonfire Night because it's special.

Marcie-Rae Moore (6)
Barcroft Primary School, Barcroft

Autumn Senses

I can see leaves fall on the ground
I can see colours all around
I can hear crunching of nuts and leaves
I can hear the wind moaning in the trees
I can smell the smoke of the fire
I can smell the BBQ wings
I can taste the delicious hot dogs
I can taste a chocolate log
I can touch the shiny conkers
Autumn is driving me bonkers.

Hannah Smith, Amolar, Keagan & Zain
Barcroft Primary School, Barcroft

My Bonfire Night Poem

B onfire night brings people together
O n bonfire night people celebrate with fireworks
N ever go near a fire because it will burn you
F ires are deadly because it will kill you
I think bonfire night is special
R ainbow is my favourite bonfire
E very autumn bonfire night is celebrated.

Sahid Mohamed (6)
Barcroft Primary School, Barcroft

My Bonfire Night Sense Poem

I can hear crackling wood
While I'm playing in the mud
I can see fireworks in the mystical sky
And they're zooming fast and high
I'm drinking refreshing Coke
And smelling all the smoke
I can taste food
Come to me if you are in the mood
I can touch sparklers all around
I can touch frost all around.

Louie Porter (7)
Barcroft Primary School, Barcroft

Autumn Senses

I can see bare branches
Snow? What are the chances?
I can hear the leaves crunching
On my toffee apple I am munching
I can smell the rain
Causing beautiful images in my brain
I can touch my cosy gloves
That is something everyone loves
I can taste a toffee apple
Whilst I hear the fire crackle.

Amy Fox (7), Jayden, Codie & Charlie
Barcroft Primary School, Barcroft

My Bonfire Night Poem

B onfire Night is special because we celebrate
O n Bonfire Night everyone comes together
N ever go near the bonfire
F ires are bad because if you go in you will die
I like the colourful fireworks
R ed fireworks are bright
E very Bonfire Night everybody has fun.

Amarpreet Singh Dhillon (6)
Barcroft Primary School, Barcroft

Autumn Sense Poem

I can see bare branches
What are the chances of rain today?
I can hear leaves crunching
While I'm munching my toffee apple
I can smell the rain
While I'm in pain
I can touch the branches
While my mam uses the matches
I can taste my apple
While my friends have a Star Wars battle.

Charley Jay Nutting (7)
Barcroft Primary School, Barcroft

My Bonfire Night Sense Poem

I can touch my warm soft gloves
Because sparklers are made out of wood
I can hear crackling wood
While I play in the mud
I can see fireworks in the mystical sky
And they're zooming fast and high
I can taste BBQ meat
It was sweet
I can smell smoke
And it is really gross.

Sol Simpson-Pratt (7)
Barcroft Primary School, Barcroft

My Bonfire Night Poem

B onfires are bright
O n Bonfire Night I feel happy
N ever go too close to the bonfire
F ireworks are so pretty
I enjoy bonfires because there are lots of colours
R ainbow fireworks are my favourite
E very time I see a bonfire I smile a lot.

Dylan Carless (6)
Barcroft Primary School, Barcroft

Bonfire Night

B onfire Night has fireworks
O n Bonfire Night my friends come over
N ovember is when Bonfire Night happens
F ireworks explode on Bonfire Night
I love Bonfire Night
R emember to be nice on Bonfire Night
E verything is fun on Bonfire Night.

Zahara Lewis-Coombs (7)
Barcroft Primary School, Barcroft

My Bonfire Night Sense Poem

I love wearing my warm, soft gloves
I can hear the crackling wood
While I play in the mud
I can see fireworks in the mystical night sky
And they are zooming fast and high
I can smell smoke in the air
And I can see the oak on the trees
I can taste air in my mouth with my food.

Elsie Richardson (7)
Barcroft Primary School, Barcroft

Bonfire Night

B onfire Night has pink fireworks
O n Bonfire Night I have my PJs on
N ovember is Bonfire Night
F ireworks are dangerous
I like my PJs on
R oaring flames are keeping us warm
E xcellent fireworks banging everywhere.

Lottie Parkes (6)
Barcroft Primary School, Barcroft

Bonfire Night

B onfire Night has big fires
O n Bonfire Night I have an orange juice
N ovember the 5th is when Bonfire Night happens
F ireworks are dangerous
I see lots of fireworks
R emember to keep safe
E very year it is here.

Hannah Connell (6)
Barcroft Primary School, Barcroft

My Bonfire Sense Poem

I can hear crackling wood
While I'm playing in the mud
I can see fireworks
They are zooming fast and high
I can taste sweet meat
I can feel gloves on my hand
While I swish my sparkler around
I can smell smoke
It makes me choke.

Tyler Evans (7)
Barcroft Primary School, Barcroft

Bonfire Night

F estival of lights
I see lights
R aining colours
E verybody is excited
W e're shouting
O n the night sky
R aining lights
K ids are happy.

Danielle Ansere (7)
Barcroft Primary School, Barcroft

Autumn Senses

I can see the leaves falling off the branches
I can hear the leaves crunching
On my toffee apple I am munching
I can smell the rain
Causing beautiful images in my brain
I can touch my cosy gloves.

Rhylee Yeend (8)
Barcroft Primary School, Barcroft

Bonfire Night

B onfire Night,
O n Bonfire Night I have fun in
N ovember
F ireworks flaming
I n the sky
R emember to be safe
E very year on Bonfire Night.

Kal Read (6)
Barcroft Primary School, Barcroft

My Bonfire Night Sense Poem

I can see the enormous blazing fireworks
I can smell the large smoky bonfire
I can touch the woolly blue gloves
I can taste the burning hot food
I can hear the blue large fireworks bang.

Logan Olivier (7)
Barcroft Primary School, Barcroft

My Bonfire Night Poem

I can see the rainbow fireworks
I can hear the fireworks exploding in the night
I can feel the wind blowing
I can taste the warm hot dogs
I can smell the smoke.

Olivia Smith (6)
Barcroft Primary School, Barcroft

My Bonfire Night Poem

I can see lots of colourful fireworks
I can hear fireworks banging
I can feel the heat from the bonfire
I can see the sparks landing
I can smell smoke.

Jack Grainger (6)
Barcroft Primary School, Barcroft

Autumn Senses

I can see pretty fireworks
I can smell fancy chicken wings
I can taste chicken nuggets Happy Meal
I can hear popping pops
I can touch the bonfire.

Dedan Abdullah (7)
Barcroft Primary School, Barcroft

My Bonfire Night Sense Poem

I can see powerful fireworks
I can smell the delicious food
I can touch banging fireworks
I can taste delicious food
I can hear banging fireworks.

Keiton Durbin (7)
Barcroft Primary School, Barcroft

Autumn Senses

I can see branches
I can hear crackling
I can smell rain and fire
I can smell fire crackling
I can touch gloves
I can taste toffee apple.

Frankie Rathbone (7)
Barcroft Primary School, Barcroft

Bonfire Night

I hear fireworks in the sky
Raining light
Festival of light
Raining water
Excited
Bright fireworks
Colours
Whoosh.

Juvraj Nijjar (6)
Barcroft Primary School, Barcroft

My Bonfire Night Poem

I can see beautiful fireworks
I can feel the sparks from the sparklers when I am wearing my gloves
I can taste candyfloss
I can smell smoke.

Carson Tipper (6)
Barcroft Primary School, Barcroft

Bonfire Night

I can see blazing fireworks
I can smell the smoky fire
I can touch red hot food
I can taste hot food
I can hear loud fireworks.

Ethan Hirst (7)
Barcroft Primary School, Barcroft

Bonfire Night

I can see smoke
I can hear and see fireworks zooming
I can feel the food in my mouth
I can smell fire
I can taste food.

Avnit Kaur (6)
Barcroft Primary School, Barcroft

My Bonfire Night Sense Poem

I can see blazing fireworks
I can smell the smoky bonfire
I can touch sparklers
I can taste food
I can hear bangs.

Aston Spittle (7)
Barcroft Primary School, Barcroft

My Bonfire Night Sense Poem

I can see bright fireworks
I can smell the smoky bonfire
I can touch sparklers
I can taste food
I can hear bangs.

Lexi-Mae Dams-Jesson (7)
Barcroft Primary School, Barcroft

Bonfire Night

I can see lights
I can hear big fireworks
I can smell delicious hot chocolate and marshmallows
I can taste chocolate.

Amelia Zaman (6)
Barcroft Primary School, Barcroft

My Bonfire Night Poem

I can see orange fireworks
I can hear a big bang
I can feel the cold
I can taste hot dogs
I can smell the fire.

Leo Short (6)
Barcroft Primary School, Barcroft

My Bonfire Night Poem

I can hear big bangs
I can see orange fire
I can feel the cold
I can taste hot dogs
I can smell the fireworks.

Paige Barham (6)
Barcroft Primary School, Barcroft

My Bonfire Night Poem

I can see fire
I can hear fireworks
I can feel my warm gloves
I can taste a hot dog
I can smell smoke.

Thomas Watkiss (7)
Barcroft Primary School, Barcroft

Bonfire Night

I can hear fireworks
I can see lots of cake
I can taste yummy chocolate cake
I can smell delicious food.

Sanaz Nahavandi-Nejad (6)
Barcroft Primary School, Barcroft

My Bonfire Night Poem

I can see colourful fireworks
I can hear big bangs
I can feel gloves
I can taste candyfloss.

Alexandra Tolley (6)
Barcroft Primary School, Barcroft

Bonfire Night

I can see the food and the fireworks
I can hear the bangs
I can smell food
I can taste food.

Junior Smith (6)
Barcroft Primary School, Barcroft

Bonfire Night

I can see fireworks
I can hear bangs
I can smell smoke
I can taste hot chocolate.

Mia Rattu (6)
Barcroft Primary School, Barcroft

Bonfire Night

I can see fireworks and fire
I can hear bangs
I can taste food
I can smell smoke.

Layliia Bolding (6)
Barcroft Primary School, Barcroft

Bonfire Night

I can see fireworks
I can hear bangs
I can taste hot chocolate
I can smell smoke.

Bobby Guy (6)
Barcroft Primary School, Barcroft

Bonfire Night

I can see lights
I can hear bangs
I can taste hot chocolate
I can smell smoke.

Casey Richards (6), Chahat & Cruz
Barcroft Primary School, Barcroft

Fluffy Friend

I am soft and coloured white
I have two pointy teeth sticking out
I like carrots and vegetables and leaves
I jump and hop a lot
What am I?

Answer: A rabbit.

Amber Warren (6)
Bishops Itchington Primary School, Bishops Itchington

Racing Car

R amp
A rena
C areful turns
I nteresting
N oisy
G oes quickly

C ool
A ction
R acing track.

Flynn Boothe (6)
Bishops Itchington Primary School, Bishops Itchington

Fish Fiend

I am black and white
I have an orange beak
I can swim very fast
I like fish
I dive deep
What am I?

Answer: A penguin.

Orri Wiles (7)
Bishops Itchington Primary School, Bishops Itchington

Cute And Fluffy

I am fluffy and cute
I have white long ears
I like carrots and grass
I hop around
What am I?

Answer: A rabbit.

Tia Hampson (7)
Bishops Itchington Primary School, Bishops Itchington

Greatest Of Them All

Q uite amazing
U se all the crowd
E xcellent musicians
E xciting rock music
N ever be disappointed.

Arlo Nateghi (6)
Bishops Itchington Primary School, Bishops Itchington

Smelly And Squeaky

I am smooth and pink
I have a curly tail
I like rolling in the mud
I oink a lot
What am I?

Answer: A pig.

Justina Tagg-Wilkinson (6)
Bishops Itchington Primary School, Bishops Itchington

What Am I?

I am happy and cute
I have a trunk
I like drinking water
I trumpet
What am I?

Answer: An elephant.

Emily Cooper (6)
Bishops Itchington Primary School, Bishops Itchington

Beware!

M arvellous
O utside
N oisy
S ee me roar
T ruck
E xcellent
R apid.

Josh Rycroft (6)
Bishops Itchington Primary School, Bishops Itchington

Fierce Poem

I am a predator
I have very sharp claws
I like having lots of teeth
I am fierce
What am I?

Austin Jenkins (6)
Bishops Itchington Primary School, Bishops Itchington

An American

I am famous and American
I have white hair
I like bossing people about
I walk
What am I?

Benjamin Watson (7)
Bishops Itchington Primary School, Bishops Itchington

A Riddle

I am cunning and fast
I have a crown
I like bananas
I have a gold tummy
What am I?

Ben Allen (7)
Bishops Itchington Primary School, Bishops Itchington

My Pet

D ogs are fluffy and cute
O ff I go across the fields
G rowls and barks.

Emily Mann (6)
Bishops Itchington Primary School, Bishops Itchington

Furry Friend

I am soft
I have a funny tail
I like to sing
I am a silly robot
What am I?

Iris Coleman (7)
Bishops Itchington Primary School, Bishops Itchington

Smooth Fur

I'm a big dog
I have spots
I like treats
I run
What am I?

Sophie Abbott (6)
Bishops Itchington Primary School, Bishops Itchington

Mickey Mouse

Mickey Mouse is lovely
Mickey Mouse is fluffy
Mickey Mouse is funny.

Jacob Brooks (6)
Bishops Itchington Primary School, Bishops Itchington

Spider-Man

Spider-Man is a superhero
Spider-Man is brave
Spider-Man is helpful.

Mason Brooks (6)
Bishops Itchington Primary School, Bishops Itchington

Autumn

Birds tweeting in the trees as they relax in the breeze
The birds tweeting in the trees as I watch them play with the bees
I can feel pumpkins on Halloween night
I can taste the food
I can taste pumpkin pie on Halloween night.

River Ackerman (6)
Hollinsclough CE Academy, Buxton

Autumn

A colourful leaf
U nderneath hedgehogs are sleeping
T rees losing their leaves
U nderground badgers are sleeping
M any fireworks flashing
N uts being collected by squirrels.

Aliza Mottram (5)
Hollinsclough CE Academy, Buxton

Autumn

A utumn starts to blow
U nder chestnut trees conkers lie
T rees lose their leaves
U nder our feet leaves rustle
M arshmallows toasty and yummy
N estling animals hiding away.

Bella Ferns (7)
Hollinsclough CE Academy, Buxton

Autumn

I can smell hot food passing by the shops
I can feel the wind blowing through my hair
I can hear the birds tweeting through the trees
I can smell the hot food coming to me
I can taste yummy food curry.

River Whorton (7)
Hollinsclough CE Academy, Buxton

Autumn

I can see colourful leaves that shimmer in the sun
I can feel the bark on the tree trunk and it feels bumpy
I can hear the wind whooshing
I can smell soup and curry
I can taste the wind.

Eva Gardham (7)
Hollinsclough CE Academy, Buxton

Autumn

Conkers falling from chestnut trees
Wind thrashing against my clothes
Leaves are crunching under my feet
Hot food drifting through the night air
Hot chocolate drifting down my throat.

Rory Wale (6)
Hollinsclough CE Academy, Buxton

Autumn

A utumn winds blow
U nder my feet leaves crunch
T oasty treats I eat
U nder trees conkers lie
M arshmallows toasting
N esting animals.

Caleb Bates (5)
Hollinsclough CE Academy, Buxton

Autumn

A utumn leaves
U nderground animals hide
T rees blowing in the wind
U nder trees conkers lie
M arshmallows toasting
N esting animals.

Buddy Searle (5)
Hollinsclough CE Academy, Buxton

Autumn

I can see leaves falling down through the air
I can smell lovely marshmallows
I can taste Halloween sweets
I can hear the whistling wind
I can feel the crunchy leaves.

Lochie Dunne-Larsen (7)
Hollinsclough CE Academy, Buxton

Autumn

I can see the fresh conkers
I can feel the wind blowing my hair
I can taste the fresh pumpkin pie
I can smell the hazelnut trees
I can see squirrels with their acorns.

Molly Marsh (8)
Hollinsclough CE Academy, Buxton

Autumn

I can feel the wind blowing in my face
I can see conkers falling from conker trees
I can hear the wind blowing
I can taste pie
I can smell pumpkin pie.

Bruno Searle (6)
Hollinsclough CE Academy, Buxton

Autumn

See the clouds moving
Feel the bumpy trees on your hands
Hear the animals rustling in the leaves
Smell the fresh nature
Taste the yummy pumpkins.

Harry Lager (7)
Hollinsclough CE Academy, Buxton

Autumn

I can see brown conkers fall from trees
White marshmallows in hot chocolate
Pink fireworks in the sky
Animals like spiky hedgehogs come out.

Indigo Grindon (6)
Hollinsclough CE Academy, Buxton

Autumn

A leaf falls
Under my feet, *crunch*
Trees waving
Umbrellas keep us dry
Munching on marshmallows
Night-time fireworks.

Hendrix Sutherland (5)
Hollinsclough CE Academy, Buxton

Autumn

I see orange pumpkins
I hear loud fireworks
I smell delicious pumpkin pie
I feel crunchy leaves
I taste yummy sweets.

Dylan Sutherland (7)
Hollinsclough CE Academy, Buxton

Autumn

I can see fresh fruit getting harvested
Feel leaves falling gently
Hear leaves crunching below my feet
Taste candy.

Rosalie Whorton (7)
Hollinsclough CE Academy, Buxton

Making Sense Of Autumn

I can hear the big trees banging against the breeze
The leaves are getting crunchy and light
I can even hear them in the deep dark night
I can hear the racing rain on my hood
I can see the lashing leaves coming my way
And a little bit of pollen floating away
I can see a red rosy firework in the beautifully black sky
I can touch the beautifully bronzed pinecone
I can smell the savage smoky bonfire under the windy willows
I can taste the dreamy delightful hot chocolate on the table by the farmer's house.

Amélie Hutchinson (6)
Malvern Parish CE Primary School, Malvern

Making Sense Of Autumn

I can hear the fighting flames of the fireworks.
I can hear branches swaying in the whistling wind.
I can see the silly salmon playing in the stream.
I can smell the tasty toasty hot chocolate on a frosty morning in my bed.
I can taste the heavy hot chocolate.
I can see the raging wind in the air.
I can taste the sweet sugary hot chocolate on a colourful day.
I can see some leaves coming my way and a little bit of pollen floating away.

Edie Morse (7)
Malvern Parish CE Primary School, Malvern

Making Sense Of Autumn

I can touch bumpy bronze pinecones
I can hear the fierce fast fireworks
I can hear the leaves crunching and waving
I can see the brave bare tree
I can see the scared scarecrow
I can see a black brave crow
I can smell strong smoke burning
I can taste the creamy cosy hot chocolate, mmm!
I can see the silly squirrels
I can hear rain pitter-patter on my head.

Hannah Nealon (6)
Malvern Parish CE Primary School, Malvern

Making Sense Of Autumn

I can touch the crunchy crispy leaves
I can hear the courageous colourful leaves falling on the forest floor
I can smell the smoky bonfire in the farmer's field in the deep dark night
I can taste the creamy comforting hot chocolate
I can see the scampering squirrels nibbling their acorns
I can hear the courageous colourful leaves falling on the forest floor.

Rosie Kelland (6)
Malvern Parish CE Primary School, Malvern

Making Sense Of Autumn

I can touch the prickly pointy pinecones
I can hear the pattering pittering rain on my window
I can see the scary scarecrow playing in the backyard
I can smell the roaring ravenous bonfire in the sooty stove
I can taste the smooth soothing hot chocolate in my bed
I can smell the smelly savage bonfire in the deep dark field.

Jamie Atkins (6)
Malvern Parish CE Primary School, Malvern

Making Sense Of Autumn

I can touch the freezing fierce icing in my ice cup in the bedroom
I can hear the pitter-patter on my umbrella, the rain is fast
I can see the deep dark forest
I can touch the fierce freezing ice
I can smell the smelly savage bonfire in my grassy green garden
I can taste the sweet smooth hot chocolate on the sofa.

Emily Lewis (7)
Malvern Parish CE Primary School, Malvern

Making Sense Of Autumn

I can touch the freezing ferocious frost
I can hear the heavy howling raindrops falling from the great grey sky
I can see a smart scarecrow playing party tricks on careless crows
I can smell the dangerous deadly bonfire in the crunchy colourful wood
I can taste the sweet smooth hot chocolate in the deep dark night.

Andrew Marlow (6)
Malvern Parish CE Primary School, Malvern

Making Sense Of Autumn

I can touch the bumpy bronzed pinecones
I can touch the freezing ferocious frost
I can hear the pitter-pattering on my hair
I can see the bendy bare branches waving at me
I can smell the smoky strong bonfire in the farmer's field in the deep dark night
I can taste the smooth singing hot chocolate.

Abigail Whiteman (6)
Malvern Parish CE Primary School, Malvern

Making Sense Of Autumn

I can touch the bumpy bronze pinecones
I can hear the racing rain pitter-patter on my misty window
I can see the courageous colourful leaves falling from the brave tree
I can smell the smoky strong bonfire in the farmer's field in the deep dark night
I can taste the mighty sweet warming hot chocolate.

George Collier (6)
Malvern Parish CE Primary School, Malvern

Making Sense Of Autumn

I can touch the bumpy bronze pinecone
I can touch the crunchy crispy leaves
I can smell the dangerous deadly bonfire in the crunchy colourful woods
I can taste the creamy comforting hot chocolate and a frightfully freezing autumn morning
I can hear the roaring raindrops
I can see the bare branches.

Edith Dolphin (6)
Malvern Parish CE Primary School, Malvern

Making Sense Of Autumn

I can smell the burning blazing bonfire out of my window
I can taste the smooth sweet hot chocolate on my bed
I can touch the pointy prickly pinecone
I can hear the heavy howling raindrops falling from the sky
I can see scampering squirrels hiding their nuts in the autumn trees.

Estella Nutt (6)
Malvern Parish CE Primary School, Malvern

Making Sense Of Autumn

I can touch the pointy prickly pinecone
I can hear the heavy howling raindrops on my window
I can see the scampering squirrels getting nuts in the woods
I can smell the smoky strong bonfire in the farmer's field in the deep dark woods
I can taste the sweet hot chocolate.

Élodie Argent (6)
Malvern Parish CE Primary School, Malvern

Making Sense Of Autumn

I can hear the fierce fireworks flaming through the sky
I can see the whooshing waving tree in the wind
I can touch the crunchy crispy leaves
I can taste the soft smooth hot chocolate on a freezing frosty morning
I can smell the sooty savage bonfire in the grassy field.

Hugo Sherman (6)
Malvern Parish CE Primary School, Malvern

Making Sense Of Autumn

I can touch the crunchy crispy leaves
I can see the squirrels
I can hear the racing rain pitter-pattering on my window
I can smell the smoky bonfire in the farmer's field in the deep dark farmer's field
I can taste the sweet smooth hot chocolate in my home.

Kourtney-Jai Thackeray (7)
Malvern Parish CE Primary School, Malvern

Making Sense Of Autumn

I can smell the bonfire in the deep dark night
I can smell the roaring raging bonfire
I can touch the pointy prickly pinecone
I can taste the sweet smooth hot chocolate in my bed
I can hear the windy wind in the sky
I can see the smart scarecrow in the field.

Jenson Iley (6)
Malvern Parish CE Primary School, Malvern

Making Sense Of Autumn

I can touch the bumpy bronze pinecones
I can hear the sapphire speedy raindrops
I can see the plump pumpkins
I can smell dangerous deadly bonfire in the crunchy colourful woods
I can taste the sweet smooth hot chocolate.

James Roberts-Haggis (7)
Malvern Parish CE Primary School, Malvern

Making Sense Of Autumn

I can touch the pointy prickly pinecone
I can hear the racing rain pitter-pattering
I can see the scampering squirrels nibbling their nuts
I can smell the smoky strong bonfire
I can taste the tasty toasty hot chocolate.

Teddy Smith (6)
Malvern Parish CE Primary School, Malvern

Making Sense Of Autumn

I can touch the scratchy scary pinecone
I can hear the magic messy fireworks
I can see the racing royal scarecrow
I can smell the smoky strong bonfire in the deep dark woods
I can taste the sweet smooth hot chocolate.

Katherine Buckman (6)
Malvern Parish CE Primary School, Malvern

Making Sense Of Autumn

I can smell the smoky bonfire
I can hear the racing rain on my misty window
I can touch the pointy prickly pinecones
I can see the crunchy leaves on the floor
I can taste the hot chocolate in my cosy bedroom.

Poppy Morris (6)
Malvern Parish CE Primary School, Malvern

Making Sense Of Autumn

I can touch the crunchy crispy leaves
I can hear the rain pitter-pattering on my window
I can see the scampering squirrels nibbling their nuts
I can smell the dangerous deadly bonfire in the crunchy woods.

Josie-May Jones (6)
Malvern Parish CE Primary School, Malvern

Making Sense Of Autumn

I can see a bird
I can hear marshmallows crackling in the fire
I can taste sweet marshmallows
I can feel cold air all around me
I can smell soggy leaves
This is autumn!

Jacob Davies (6)
Malvern Parish CE Primary School, Malvern

Flames Of Fire

What a sight I saw
Screaming people running for their lives
Huge flames burning many houses rapidly
Smothering smoke spreading across the bustling humongous city
What a sight I saw
What a sound I heard
Crackling flames spreading house to house
Terrified people running for their dear lives
Such a sound I heard
Such a smell I smelled
Suffocating smoke.

Leonidas McNally (6)
Ormiston Cliff Park Primary Academy, Gorleston

Fire!

What a sight I saw
Orange flames were spreading
Rapidly it spread so fast
The wind blew
The fire got really fast
It jumped from house to house
People ran for their lives
Going to the River Thames
What a sound I heard
Terrified people screaming
People were screaming in their horse and carts.

Oreoluwa Odyneye (6)
Ormiston Cliff Park Primary Academy, Gorleston

Fire! Fire!

What a sight I saw
Red glowing flames spreading
Through the streets
What a sight I saw
The deadly smoke suffocating
Screaming people and terrified people
Orange fire rapidly
Higgledy-piggledy houses
Crackling fire
What a sight I saw.

Abdul Ahad (6)
Ormiston Cliff Park Primary Academy, Gorleston

What I Saw

What a sight I saw
Orange and red glowing flames
The higgledy-piggledy buildings
I heard horses and people
I smelled burning shops and smoke
Lots of people got sick
And people ran to the River Thames
And got on boats
What a sight I saw.

Marnie Rudkin (7)
Ormiston Cliff Park Primary Academy, Gorleston

Flickering Flames

Such a sight I saw
Dangerous boiling flames burning through the streets
Terrified people fleeing to the safe River Thames
Large clouds of poisonous smoke
Such a sight I saw
Such a sound I heard
Suffocating flames tear through every building.

Lyla Puszczewicz (6)
Ormiston Cliff Park Primary Academy, Gorleston

Flickering Flames

Such a sight I saw
Suffocating flames burning
Through the rectangular streets
Petrified people fleeing to the safe River Thames
Large clouds of poisonous smoke
Such a sound I heard
Dangerous flames tear through every building.

Ross Vaudin (6)
Ormiston Cliff Park Primary Academy, Gorleston

The Raging Fire

Such a sight I saw
The people were petrified because of the fire
Flames burning the wooden houses
The fire grew bigger and bigger
The people got shocked
Terrified people scared of the fire and flames
The fire burnt down 700 houses.

Yalini Manivannan (6)
Ormiston Cliff Park Primary Academy, Gorleston

London's Burning

What a sight I saw
The fire spread rapidly
I could see people running rapidly
I could see wooden houses

Murderous orange flames attacking
The capital city, London
The fire was deadly
The houses were higgledy-piggledy.

Henry Cutchey (6)
Ormiston Cliff Park Primary Academy, Gorleston

Flickering Flames

Such a sight I saw
Sizzling flames burning through the orange fire
Burning people fleeing to the River Thames
Large clouds of rocky smoke
Such a sight I saw
Such a sound I heard
Big flames tearing through every building.

Harper Leigh (6)
Ormiston Cliff Park Primary Academy, Gorleston

The Great Fire Of London

Such a sight I saw
Roasting flames burning through
Terrified people fleeing to the River Thames
Large clouds of choking thick smoke
Such a sight I saw
Such a sound I heard
Crackling flames burning through every building.

Lewis Wright (6)
Ormiston Cliff Park Primary Academy, Gorleston

Flames That Spread

What a sight I saw
Terrifying burning hot flames
Rapidly burning down wooden houses
Suffocating grey smoke killing people
Dangerous orange and red flames
Rapidly burning down houses through the city
What a sight I saw.

Iris Rogers
Ormiston Cliff Park Primary Academy, Gorleston

What A Sight I Saw

Such a sight I saw
Scorching and life-threatening flames
Jumping from house to house
Hundreds of wooden houses being burnt to ashes
Hundreds of terrified people running rapidly
To the River Thames
Such a sight I saw.

Mason Sandry (6)
Ormiston Cliff Park Primary Academy, Gorleston

The Flickering Flames

Such a sight I saw
Spreading flames burning through the bumpy streets
Petrified people fleeing to the safe River Thames
Large clouds of poisonous smoke
Such a sight I saw
Such a sound I heard
Angry flames tearing.

Freddie Roden (6)
Ormiston Cliff Park Primary Academy, Gorleston

Flickering Flames

Such a sight I saw
Boiling flames burning through the cobbled streets
Petrified people fleeing to the safe River Thames
Large clouds of blinding smoke
Such a sight I saw
Sizzling flames tear through every building.

Jenson Brooks (6)
Ormiston Cliff Park Primary Academy, Gorleston

The Raging Fire

Such a sight I saw
Flames burning through the streets
Terrified people fleeing to the River Thames
Large clouds of grey smoke billowing
Such a sound I heard
Crackling flames burning through every building.

Joanna Mercy Jomy (6)
Ormiston Cliff Park Primary Academy, Gorleston

Flickering Flames

Such a sight I saw
The people were going to find a safe space
Angry flames burning through the bumpy tight streets
To the safe River Thames
Large clouds of blinding smoke
Such a sight I saw.

Isaac Bartram (6)
Ormiston Cliff Park Primary Academy, Gorleston

Flickering Flames

Such a sight I saw
Orange flames burning through the rocky streets
Terrified people fleeing to the safe River Thames
The clouds of poisonous smoke
Such a sight I saw
Such a sound I heard.

Roma Down (7)
Ormiston Cliff Park Primary Academy, Gorleston

London Flames

What a sight I saw
Monstrous fires destroying the higgledy-piggledy houses
Black suffocating smoke billowing out the wooden houses
What a sight I saw
Terrified people screaming and burning.

Leon Quelch
Ormiston Cliff Park Primary Academy, Gorleston

The Great Fire Of London

Such a sight I saw
Burning flames, dancing flames
Burning the houses
Scared people running for their lives
Samuel Pepys rowing the boat
Samuel Pepys escaped from the Fire of London.

Thomas Russell (6)
Ormiston Cliff Park Primary Academy, Gorleston

Flickering Flames

Such a sight I saw
Furious flames burning through the tight streets
Petrified people fleeing to the safe River Thames
Large clouds of smoke
Such a sight I saw
Such a sound I heard.

Grace Chance (7)
Ormiston Cliff Park Primary Academy, Gorleston

The Worst Fire

Dancing flames and choking black smoke
Speechless people fleeing to the River Thames
Large clouds of deadly black smoke drifting
Flames popping like popcorn
Burning through every building.

Anna Haziri (6)
Ormiston Cliff Park Primary Academy, Gorleston

Raging Fire

Such a sight I saw
Roasting yellow flames
Burning through wooden houses
Scared people fleeing to the River Thames
Larger clouds of thick dancing orange smoke
Such a sight I saw.

Ezmai Doroba (6)
Ormiston Cliff Park Primary Academy, Gorleston

The Great Fire

Such a sight I saw
I saw red-hot flames burning through London
I saw petrified people fleeing for their lives to the River Thames
Large clouds of smoke drifting
Such a sight I saw.

Sienna (6)
Ormiston Cliff Park Primary Academy, Gorleston

The Great Fire Of London

Such a sight I saw
Yellow flames burning through the black street
Scared people fleeing to the River Thames
Large clouds of thick black dancing orange smoke
Such a sight I saw.

Nour Genena (6)
Ormiston Cliff Park Primary Academy, Gorleston

Flickering Flames

Such a sight I saw
Colossal flames burning through the sizzling streets
Frightened people fleeing to the safe River Thames
Large clouds of boiling smoke
Such a sight I saw.

Arya Vikramraj (6)
Ormiston Cliff Park Primary Academy, Gorleston

The Fire Of London

Such a sight I saw
Red flames burning through ruined streets
Petrified people fleeing to the River Thames
Large clouds of thick grey smoke drifting
Such a sight I saw.

Maya Adams (6)
Ormiston Cliff Park Primary Academy, Gorleston

Flickering Flames

Such a sight I saw
Orange flames burning through the cobbled streets
Terrified people fleeing to the safe River Thames
Large cloud of thick smoke
Such a sight I saw.

Malwina
Ormiston Cliff Park Primary Academy, Gorleston

The Flickering Flames

Such a sight I saw
Orange flames burning through the streets
People fleeing to the safe River Thames
Large clouds of poisonous smoke
Such a sight I saw.

Toby Rix (6)
Ormiston Cliff Park Primary Academy, Gorleston

Flickering Flames

Such a sight I saw
Sizzling flames burning through the long streets
Terrified people fleeing to safety
Such a sound I heard
Angry flames tearing.

Elsie Smith (6)
Ormiston Cliff Park Primary Academy, Gorleston

Fire Flames

What a sight I saw
The fire was rapidly burning the buildings
The people burning
Samuel Pepys was there
I could hear the fire crackling.

Link Mitchell (6)
Ormiston Cliff Park Primary Academy, Gorleston

London's Burning

What a sight I saw
The orange and red flames
Hot ash, sparks
The terrified people running rapidly
And the powerful wind.

Beau Learmonth (6)
Ormiston Cliff Park Primary Academy, Gorleston

The Fire

Such a sight I saw
Red yellow dancing flames
Burning through houses
Frightened people fleeing to the River Thames.

Charliee Louise Down (6)
Ormiston Cliff Park Primary Academy, Gorleston

Flickering Flames

Such a sight I saw
Sizzling flames
Burning flames
Through the rocky streets
Terrified people fleeing.

Frankie Potter (6)
Ormiston Cliff Park Primary Academy, Gorleston

Fire

I can see suffocating smoke
Fire and flickering flames
People running and shouting
Screaming for help.

Evie Redmond (6)
Ormiston Cliff Park Primary Academy, Gorleston

What I Saw

What a sight I saw
The red flames and smoke
Glowing flames and smoke
The people scared and terrified.

Ezmai Eaton (6)
Ormiston Cliff Park Primary Academy, Gorleston

What I Saw

What a sight I saw
Screaming people running for their lives
To the River Thames
What a sight I saw.

Nicola Anne (6)
Ormiston Cliff Park Primary Academy, Gorleston

Flames Of Fire

What a sight I saw
Red and orange houses were burning
Grey smoke going to the houses.

Yusuf Kadar (6)
Ormiston Cliff Park Primary Academy, Gorleston

My Autumn Senses

I can see orange, yellow, red and brown leaves, and conkers on the ground.
I can see scary pumpkins with frightening candlelight faces.
I see multicoloured sparkling fireworks.
I hear dry leaves rustling in the wind.
I hear children knocking on the door saying, "Trick or treat," and laughing.
I hear loud bangs and crackles.
I smell wet and damp leaves.
I smell the sweetness of toffee apples.
I smell bonfires burning in the smoky air.
I can taste my mum's home-made soup and dumplings.
I can taste all the yummy Halloween treats.
I can taste hot dogs with ketchup and warm chestnuts.
I feel cold in the autumn nights.
I feel cosy when I put on my autumn pyjamas.
I feel happy in autumn because Christmas is not far away.

Annalise Campbell (6)
Our Lady & St Joseph RC Primary School, Hackney

Autumn Fireworks

Boom, boom, boom... blast in the night sky
Boom, boom, boom... colourful and brightening in the eyes
All shiny, all sparkling, all special, all stunning and stimulating
The colour is stimulating and always attractive
Shining, bright stars out in the darkness
Brightening the sky, with all its boom.

Boom, boom, boom, flaming flowers come up most in October
To lighten up the autumn occasion.
Join the crew to blast fireworks
Its light is more appreciated when it is dark
But still sparkling all the time
The essence of its beauty is so positive
I am thrilled to see fireworks because it's fun and *boom!*

Tehillah Sodunke (6)
Our Lady & St Joseph RC Primary School, Hackney

I Love Autumn

In the autumn, I can see;
Brown and orange leaves dancing in the breeze.
I hear birds singing in the trees,
I also can see their nests that were hidden by the leaves.
In the autumn, I can feel
The chilly wind as cold as steel!
I smell hot chocolate in the morning;
My mama makes it to keep me warm.
It tastes so yummy in my tummy!
I like it to be thick and not too runny.
We live near a river with boats that are homes;
I smell the wood they burn to keep nice and warm.
I *love* autumn and all its smells!
I hope that now you love autumn as well!

Luca Chiromo (6)
Our Lady & St Joseph RC Primary School, Hackney

The Sweet Smell Of Autumn

I can see colourful red and orange leaves
Floating down to the ground
I can see trees waving to the sun
I can hear birds singing sweet songs
I listen to the leaves going *crunch, crunch, crunch* under my feet
I can smell the fragrant flowers while I squeeze nectar from the fuchsia
I can smell Halloween on its way
I can taste pumpkins and apples and spices, oh my!
I can feel the soft breeze on my skin as I put on a shawl
I feel as happy as jelly wiggling on a plate.

Eabha Enver (6)
Our Lady & St Joseph RC Primary School, Hackney

I Love Autumn Because...

It's a time to prepare for a change of seasons
A miracle will appear
Leaves fall down from the trees
Colours of red, yellow, orange and brown fill the ground
Crunching sound of the leaves fill the air
Animals hide till it gets warmer
Clocks go back as the days become shorter
Autumn is my favourite season of all.

Elijah Mckenzie (7)
Our Lady & St Joseph RC Primary School, Hackney

Autumn Things

I see the autumn leaves and I hear them too
They go *crunch crunch* as I walk to school
I feel the autumn breeze as I play football
On Saturday morning after a long week of school
I can taste hot chocolate, it's my favourite thing
I really love the smell, it's almost everything.

Elijah Gomez (6)
Our Lady & St Joseph RC Primary School, Hackney

My Autumn Poem

I can see my doggy Buddy playing in the leaves
That have fallen from the trees
Red, burnt orange and yellow
I can hear fireworks exploding and witches cackling
I can taste the sweet gooey porridge
I can smell dirty dusty smoke
I love all things autumn.

Ivy Neave (6)
Our Lady & St Joseph RC Primary School, Hackney

Autumn For Me

A nimals are getting ready to sleep
U mbrellas come out to play
T he leaves turn brown and fall to the ground
U nder the covers to keep warm
M ornings are bright and very cold
N ight is dark, night is dark.

Haviliah Ojarikre (6)
Our Lady & St Joseph RC Primary School, Hackney

My Conkers Sense Poem

I can see the autumn leaves falling down
I can hear conkers plopping as they hit the ground
I can feel the soft but spiky conker shell
I can taste the sweet marshmallows in my hot chocolate
I can smell the fresh-cut grass.

Evie Doyle (6)
Our Lady & St Joseph RC Primary School, Hackney

Autumn

Autumn leaves turning brown then falling down
The wind in my hair
Playing in the leaves
Feeling the chill of autumn's breath
Back to school for me
Wearing mittens and knitted hats
People making pumpkin pie.

Luca Nguyen-Finer (7)
Our Lady & St Joseph RC Primary School, Hackney

Autumn Days And Nights

I can see the leaves changing colour in the tree
I can feel the wind blowing them free
I can smell pumpkin pie
I can see the starry sky
I can taste hot chocolate with a spoon
I can hear fireworks boom.

Eliott Arnoux (7)
Our Lady & St Joseph RC Primary School, Hackney

Autumn

A utumn has lots of leaves
U p in the sky there are clouds
T he trees are brown
U nder the trees are conkers
M ornings are dark
N ice walks in the park.

Niamh Buck (7)
Our Lady & St Joseph RC Primary School, Hackney

Autumn Senses

I see orange leaves on the ground
I can smell wet dog
My nan makes me tasty hot soup with dumplings, yummy
I can hear fireworks crackling
I can feel the dry leaves
I can feel the cold.

Nathaniel Mullings-Khan (6)
Our Lady & St Joseph RC Primary School, Hackney

Bonfire Night

I feel happy and excited
I can see a nice dark sky lit with bright colours
I can hear a bang of fireworks
I can smell the burning bonfire
I can taste yummy toffee apples
I feel happy.

Luca Grossi (6)
Our Lady & St Joseph RC Primary School, Hackney

Autumn Magic

It is crunchy red, orange, yellow and brown
Wind is blowing all around
Shaped like hands, spikes and elf's ears
Branches have dropped conkers and acorns on the wet grass
What am I?

Sienna Monero (6)
Our Lady & St Joseph RC Primary School, Hackney

My Leaves Fall From Trees

I can see leaves
I can hear the rustling leaves
I can feel the wind in my face
I can taste the earthy scent of autumn
I can smell nature.

Janelle Alexander (6)
Our Lady & St Joseph RC Primary School, Hackney

What Do You Think It Is?

It is smart, it has black ears and white paws
Also, it is polite and it is happy all the time
It is never angry or mean
It also is very, very funny
Also, he likes rainbows
He always comes in my garden
I try to catch him but he runs away
What is he?

Answer: My next-door neighbour's cat!

Abdullah Khan (6)
Ribbleton Avenue Infant School, Preston

What Am I?

Even though I have no feet
I still have a boot
I can be big, I can be small
Mostly I have four doors
Some are black, some are white
I am a car.

Lewis Nuttall (6)
Ribbleton Avenue Infant School, Preston

Young Writers Information

We hope you have enjoyed reading this book – and that you will continue to in the coming years.

If you're the parent or family member of an enthusiastic poet or story writer, do visit our website www.youngwriters.co.uk/subscribe and sign up to receive news, competitions, writing challenges and tips, activities and much, much more! There's lots to keep budding writers motivated!

If you would like to order further copies of this book, or any of our other titles, then please give us a call or order via your online account.

Young Writers
Remus House
Coltsfoot Drive
Peterborough
PE2 9BF
(01733) 890066
info@youngwriters.co.uk

Join in the conversation!
Tips, news, giveaways and much more!

f YoungWritersUK   YoungWritersCW   youngwriterscw